Joy Over Your Child's Education™

The ABC's Of Sign Language

I0223453

This book utilizes the
ASL (American Sign Language) Alphabet
and
©Laugh-A-Bets artistic collections

Studies suggest that the use of sign language can be beneficial to both hearing and deaf children. Sign language relies heavily on the brain's ability to process visual imagery. ASL users tend to demonstrate faster processing ability, suggesting that it may enhance certain processing functions of the human brain (Per the National Institute on Deafness and Other Communication Disorders).

Furthermore, communication is a key ingredient in eliminating physical and cultural barriers and prejudices. Therefore exposure to this unique language can only enhance your child's perception of the world. Not to mention ASL (American Sign Language) is the third most used language in the United States next to English and Spanish!

Text copyright © 2010 by Mario A. N. Beasley.
All rights reserved.
Illustrations copyright ©Laugh-A-Bets 1997 – 2011
by Mario Beasley. All rights reserved.

ISBN 978-0-9844041-0-0

Published by Our J.O.Y.C.E. Incorporated (OJI Books division).
Joy Over Your Child's Education™ is a registered trademark
of Our J.O.Y.C.E. Incorporated

Joy Over Your Child's Education™

The ABC's Of

S I G N

Featuring ©Laugh-A-Bets

Language

Written and Illustrated by
Mario A. N. Beasley

OJI BOOKS

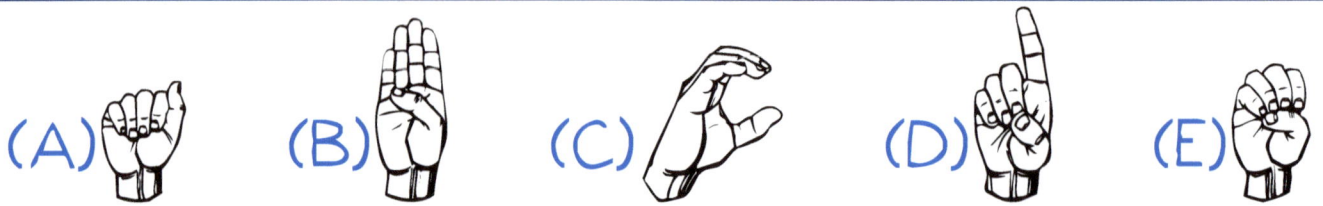

ASL (American Sign-Language)

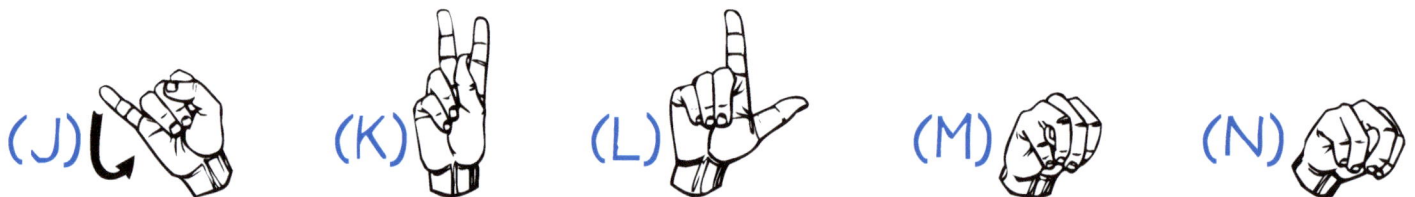

Alphabets

Aa

©Laugh-A-Bets

A _____

a _____

Bb

©Laugh-A-Bets

B

b

Cc

©Laugh-A-Bets

C _____

- -

_____

- -

c _____

Dd

©Laugh-A-Bets

D _____

d _____

Ee

©Laugh-A-Bets

E _____

e _____

F f

©Laugh-A-Bets

F _____
- -
_____

f _____
- -
_____

Gg

©Laugh-A-Bets

G _____

g _____

Hh

©Laugh-A-Bets

H _____

h _____

Ii

©Laugh-A-Bets

I

i

J j

©Laugh-A-Bets

J

j

Kk

©Laugh-A-Bets

K _____

k _____

Ll

©Laugh-A-Bets

L

l

Mm

©Laugh-A-Bets

M _____

m _____

Nn

©Laugh-A-Bets

N _____

n _____

©Laugh-A-Bets

P p

©Laugh-A-Bets

P _____

_ _

_____

p _

_____

Qq

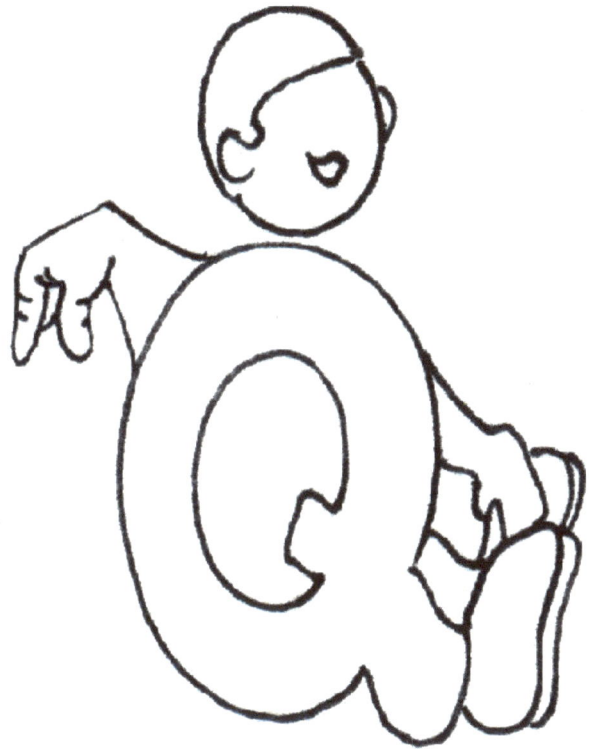

©Laugh-A-Bets

Q _____

_____

_____

_____

q _____

Rr

©Laugh-A-Bets

R _____

r _____

S s

©Laugh-A-Bets

S _____

s _____

T t

©Laugh-A-Bets

T _____
  -
  _____
t -
  _____

Uu

©Laugh-A-Bets

U

u

V v

©Laugh-A-Bets

V _____

V _____

W w

©Laugh-A-Bets

W _____

w _____

Xx

©Laugh-A-Bets

X _____

X _____

Y y

©Laugh-A-Bets

Y

Y

Zz

©Laugh-A-Bets

Z _____

_____

z --

_____

Coloring Fun

Coloring Fun

J. Mario Beasley

Coloring Fun

Purchase other exciting OJI Books and Our J.O.Y.C.E. Incorporated, Educational Tools and Apparel at:

WWW.OURJOYCE.COM

©Laugh-A-Bets and ©Sum-Joy
Infant Apparel

©Laugh-A-Bets and ©Sum-Joy
Full-size Alphabets and Numeric Posters

Customized ©Laugh-A-Bets Sign-Language Apparel

...and more to come..

www.ingramcontent.com/pod-product-compliance
Lightning Source LLC
Chambersburg PA
CBHW042012080426

42734CB00002B/55